The Joy of First Classics

Selected and edited by Denes Agay.

Foreword

The Joy of First Classics presents a colorful repertory of easy pieces by master composers, both well-known and lesser-known. Indeed, the student and player will find here numerous names and works not encountered before; music which has been unduly neglected, but deserving – because of its intrinsic musical value – to be included in the teaching repertory of the early-grade student.

The word 'classics' in our title indicates not only the style of the Viennese masters, Haydn, Mozart, Beethoven, and their contemporaries, but, in a broader sense, music which has shown itself worthy of general esteem for a considerable span of time. Certainly, works which have been known, played, and loved for a century (Liszt), or even considerably longer (Bach) qualify to be termed 'classic'.

The pieces are in their original forms. Expression marks, fingerings, were added and, in a very few cases, minor editorial adjustments made to clarify the note-picture and facilitate understanding. Keyboard miniatures of three centuries – musically rewarding and technically the most accessible – comprise the content of this volume; instructive and diverting fare for all beginning and early-grade pianists.

Denes Agay

Exclusive Distributors:
Hal Leonard
7777 West Bluemound Road,
Milwaukee, WI 53213
Email: info@halleonard.com

Hal Leonard Europe Limited
42 Wigmore Street, Marylebone,
London WIU 2RY
Email: info@halleonardeurope.com

Hal Leonard Australia Pty. Ltd.
4 Lentara Court, Cheltenham,
Victoria 9132, Australia
Email: info@halleonard.com.au

Order No. YK 21376
US International Standard Book Number: 0.8256.8066.2
UK International Standard Book Number: 0.7119.1101.0

Yorktown Music Press, Inc.

Old German Dance

Michael Praetorius
(1571 - 1621)

Canario
Old Dance

Joachim von der Hofe
(about 1612)

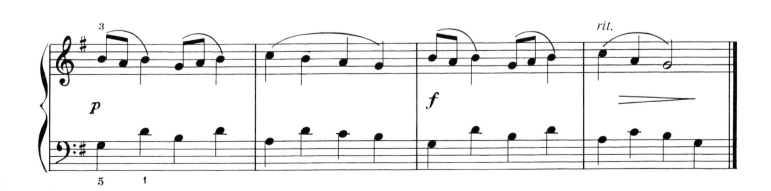

Little Sonata

1. Moderato

C. H. Wilton
(18th Century)

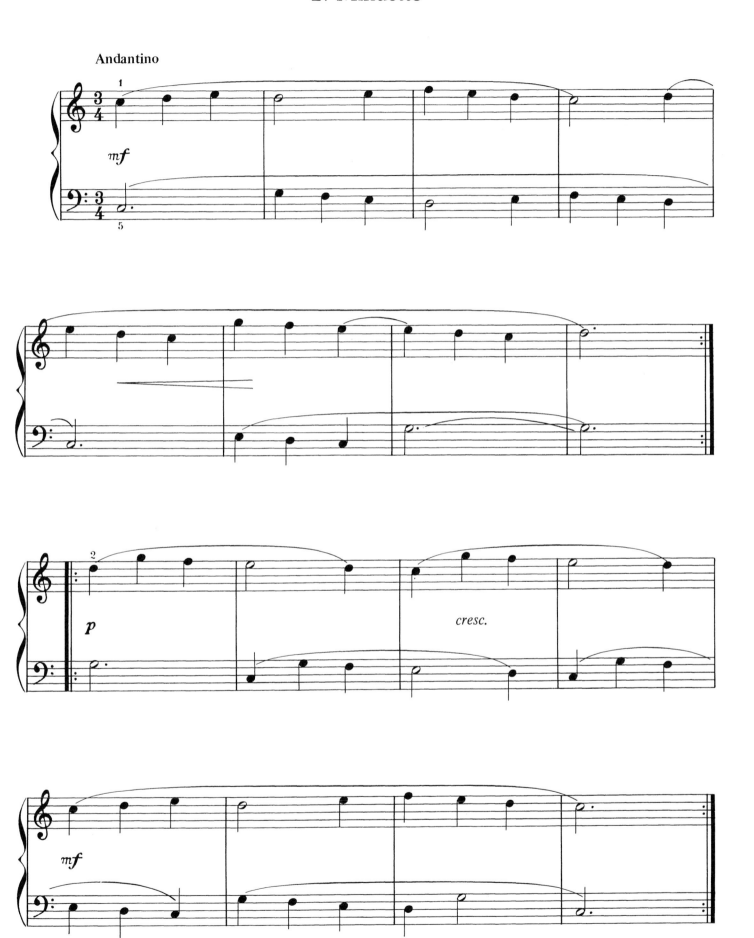

2. Minuetto

Brave Knight

Moritz Vogel
(1846 - 1922)

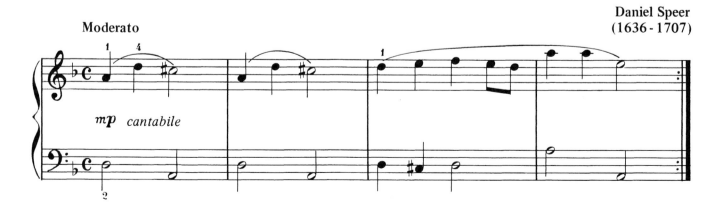

Aria

Daniel Speer
(1636 - 1707)

Follow Me!

Kálmán Chován*
(1852 - 1928)

* Pronounced KHO- vahn. Hungarian composer and influential pedagogue.

Four Little Pieces

1. Entreé

Daniel Gottlob Türk
(1756 - 1813)

Allegretto

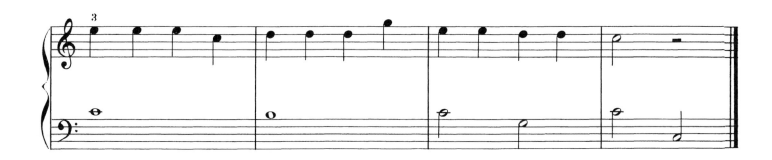

2. Minuetto

Andantino

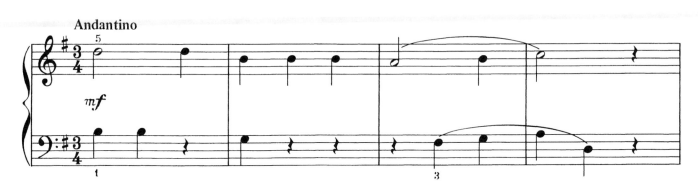

3. Complaint

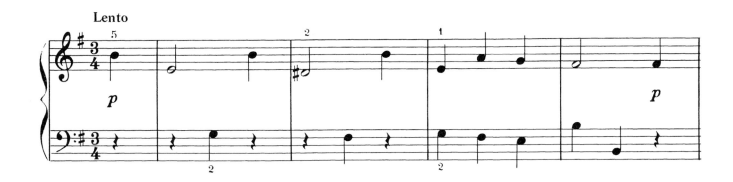

4. Carefree

Gavotte

George Frideric Handel
(1685 - 1759)

Russian Dance

Alexander Goedicke
(1877 - 1957)

Allegro moderato

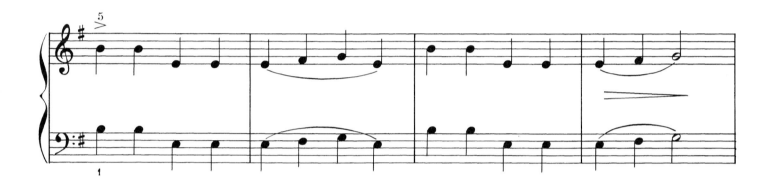

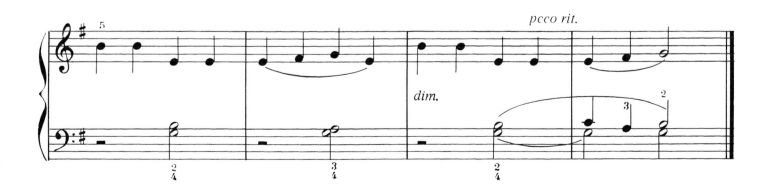

Two Little Inventions

1.

Jan Jakub Ryba*
(1765 - 1815)

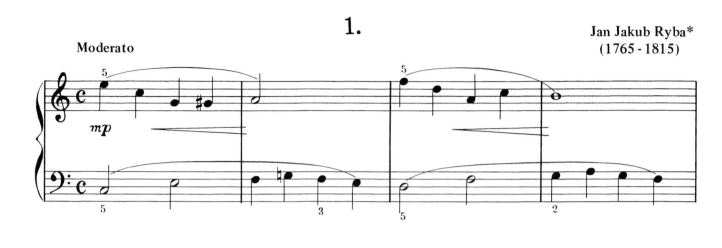

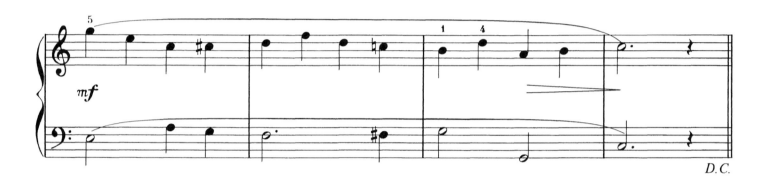

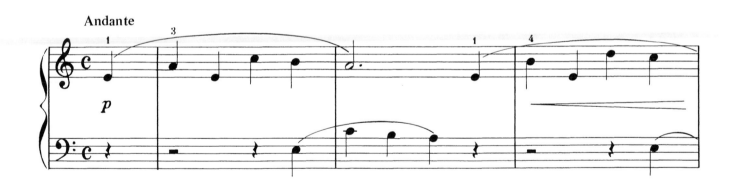

2.

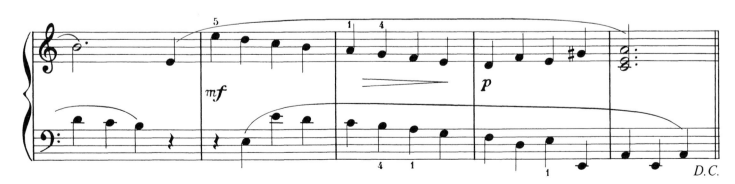

* Pronounced REE - bah. Czech composer of many works, mostly vocal.

Gavotte

Johann Georg Witthauer
(1750 - 1802)

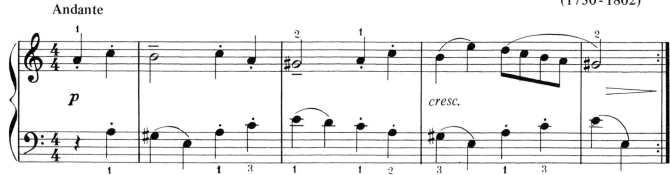

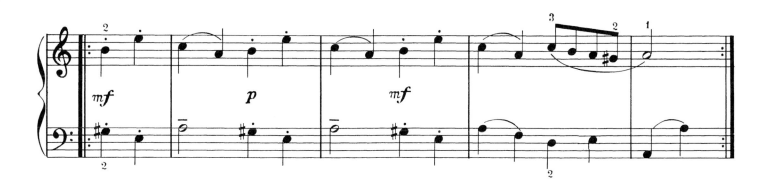

Danse Galante

Johann Georg Witthauer
(1750 - 1802)

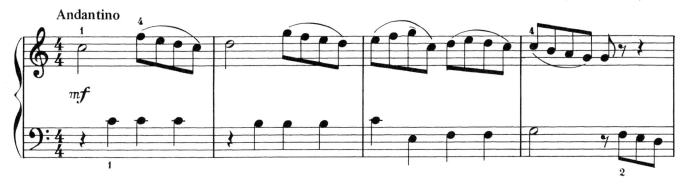

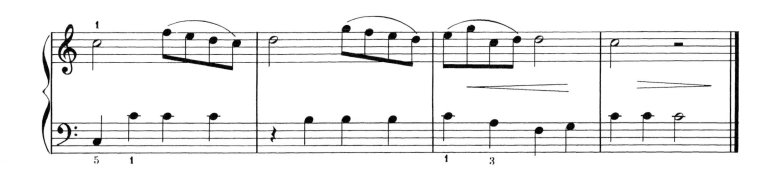

Two Hungarian Play Tunes

1.

István Bartalus
(1821 - 1899)

2.

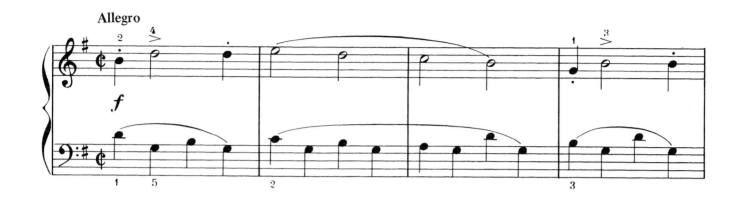

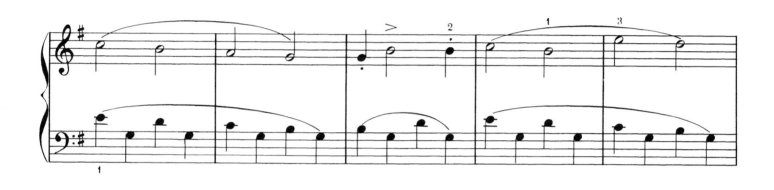

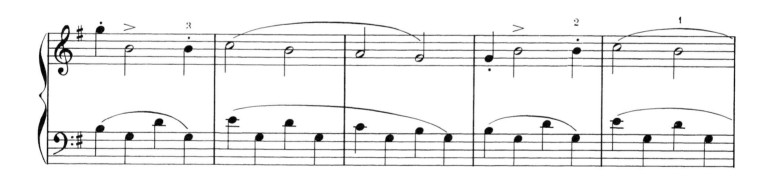

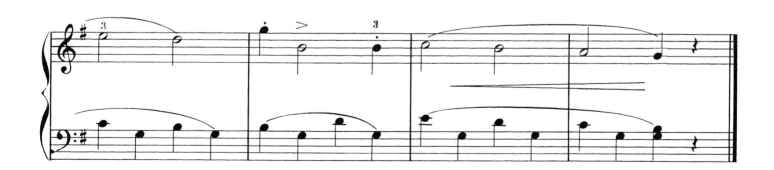

Bear Dance

from the sketch book for Album For The Young

Robert Schumann
(1810 - 1856)

The Lute Player

Bourré

Jacques Saint - Luc*
(1616 - 1689)

* Pronounced San - Lueck. Belgian composer and virtuoso on the lute.

Song Without Words

Fritz Spindler
(1817 - 1905)

Allegretto

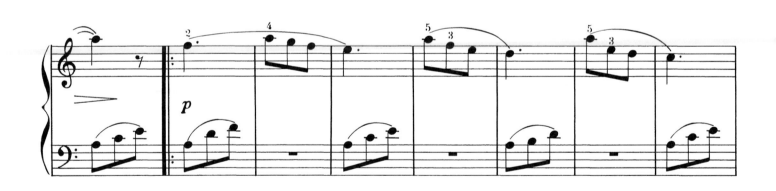

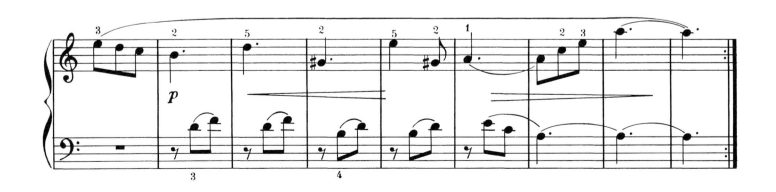

Exuberance

German Dance

Nikolaus Joseph Hüllmandel
(1751 - 1823)

Carefree Stroll

Louis Köhler
(1820 - 1886)

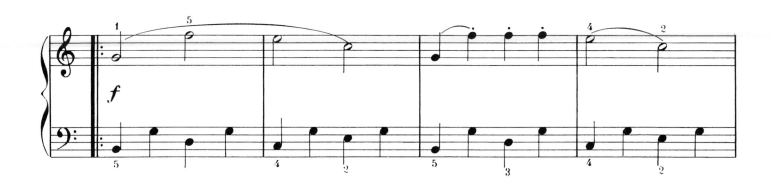

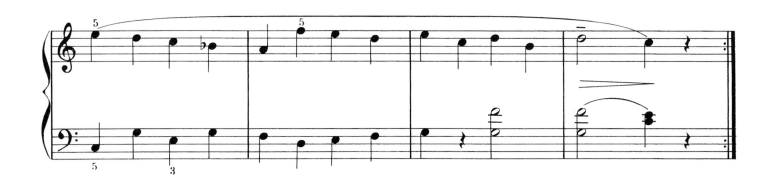

German Dance

Joseph Haydn
(1732 - 1809)

Dance Song

Sperontes (J. S. Scholze)
(1705 - 1750)

* German composer and poet. Famous lyricist and publisher of a
collection of popular dance melodies.

Duettino

Johann Wilhelm Hässler
(1747 - 1822)

Andantino

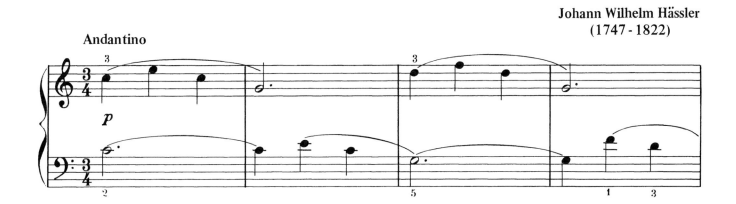

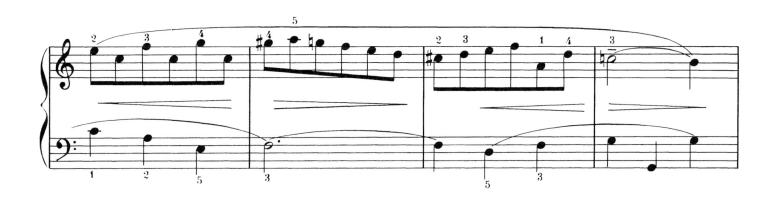

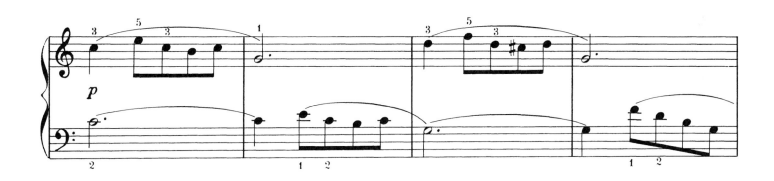

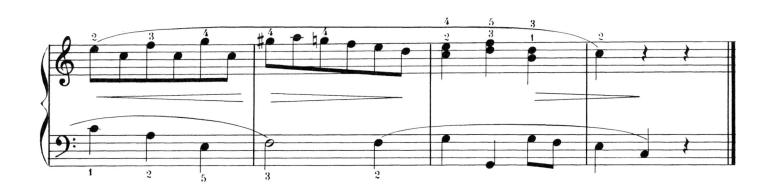

Old English Air

Felton's Gavotte

William Felton
(1713 - 1769)

Andante grazioso

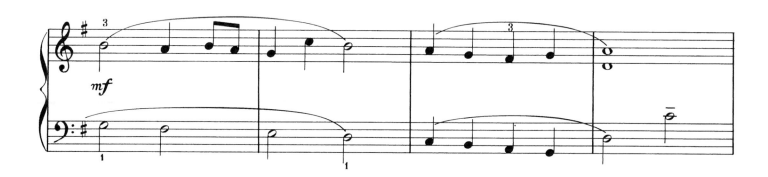

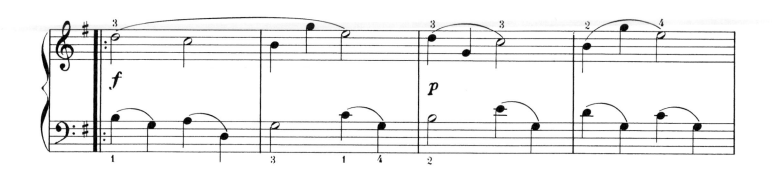

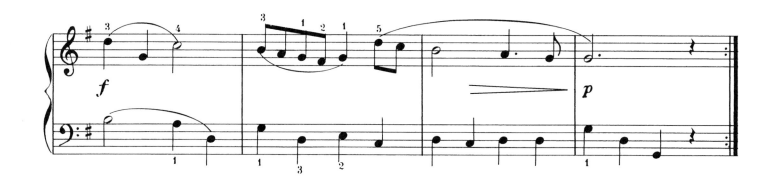

Mazurka

Maria Szymanowska *
(1790 - 1831)

* Pronounced SHEE-ma-novska. Polish piano virtuoso and composer.
  A pupil of John Field, admired by Robert Schumann.

Minuet

From the Little Notebook for
Anna Magdalena Bach ∗
(1725)

∗ Johann Sebastian Bach's second wife.

Russian Folk Song

Ludwig van Beethoven
(1770 - 1827)

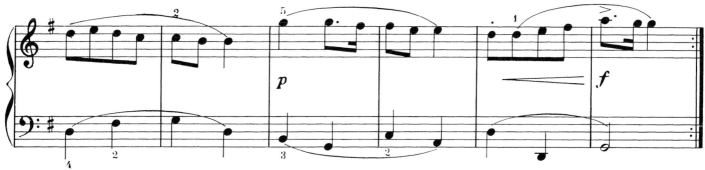

Tarantella

Scotson Clark
(1840 - 1883)

La Montagnarde

The Highland Girl

Jean Joseph Mouret
(1682 - 1738)

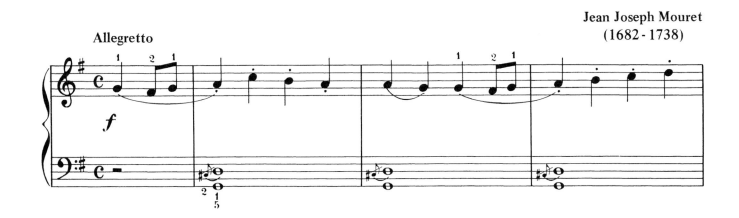

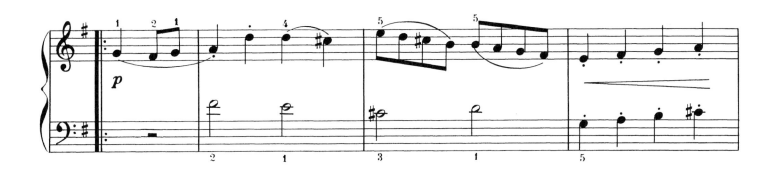

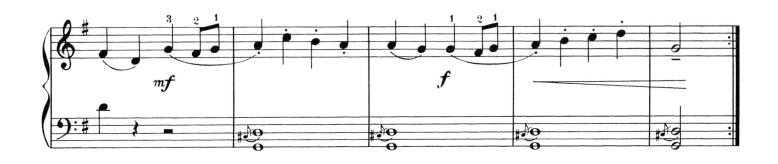

Minuet K.6

Wolfgang Amadeus Mozart
(1756 - 1791)

Andante grazioso

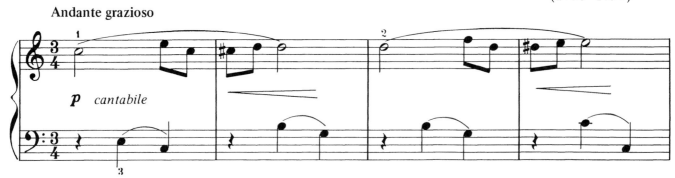

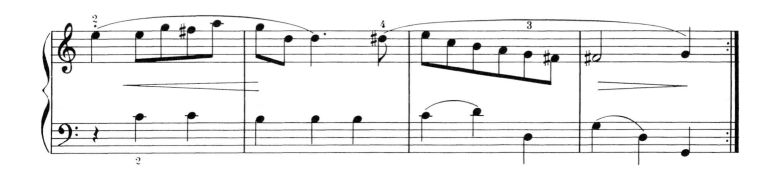

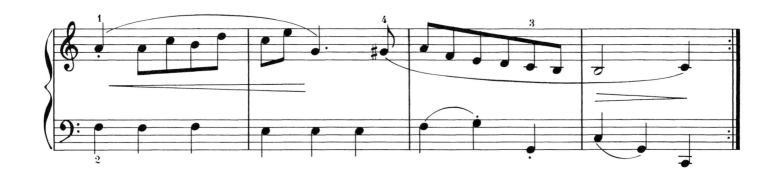

Bagatelle

Antonio Diabelli
(1781 - 1858)

Musette

From the Little Notebook for
Anna Magdelena Bach
(1725)

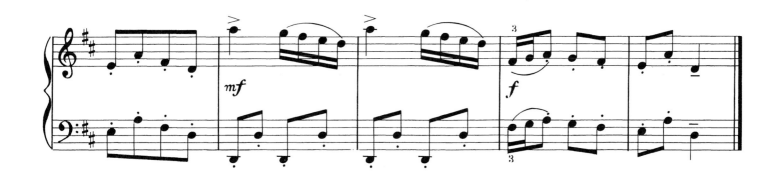

Minuet

From Leopold Mozart's *
Little Notebook for Nannerl

Andante grazioso

* *Compiled for his daughter Anna Maria, sister of Wolfgang Amadeus.*

Pastorale

Friedrich Burgmüller
(1806 - 1874)

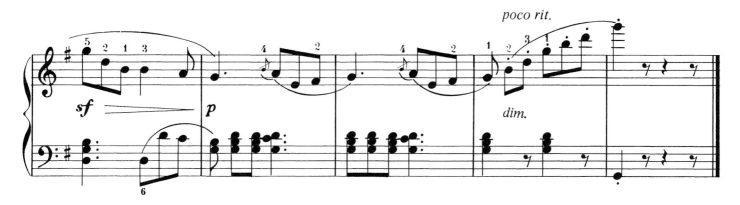

Bourrée

Johann Krieger
(1651 - 1735)

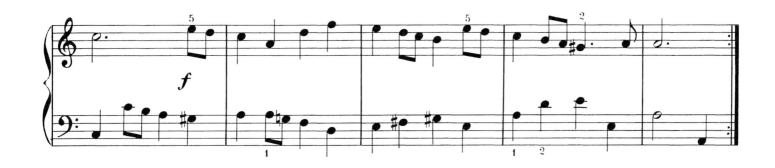

Village Dance*

Ludwig van Beethoven
(1770 - 1827)

Allegretto

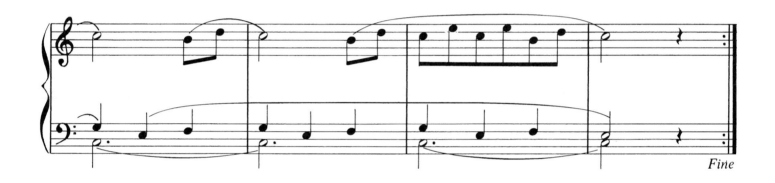

Fine

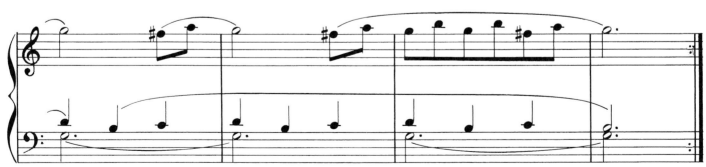

D.C. al Fine

* From one of Beethoven's sketch - books.

The Cuckoo Waltz

August Eberhard Müller
(1767 - 1817)

Mount Vernon Set

1. Intrada

Alexander Reinagle*
(1756 - 1809)

2. Promenade

* English composer and teacher who came to America in 1786. Nellie Custis, George
   Washington's adopted daughter was one of his pupils.

3. Minuet

Andantino

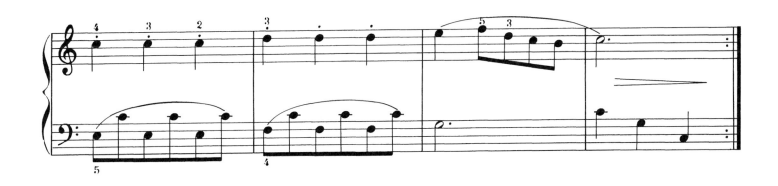

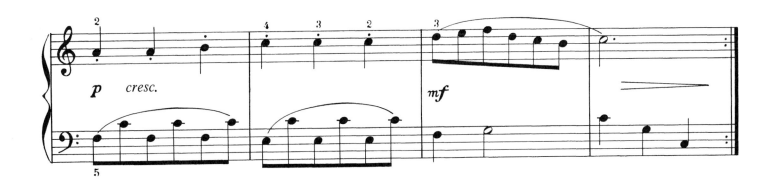

4. Quadrille

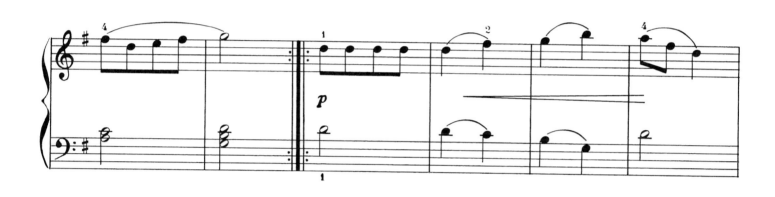

Cradle Song

Johann Philipp Kirnberger
(1721 - 1783)

Christmas Pastorale

The Shepherd's Call from Bethlehem

Valentin Rathgeber
(1682 - 1750)

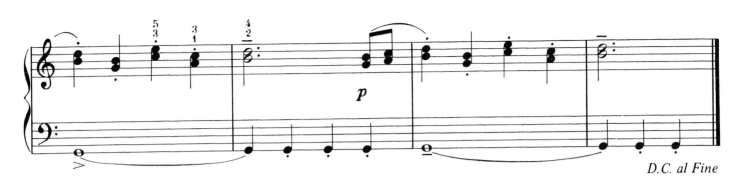

D.C. al Fine

Ecossaise

Ludwig van Beethoven
(1770 - 1827)

Arabesque

Friedrich Burgmüller

Waltz

Franz Schubert

Sonata

Minuet

Andantino

Domenico Scarlatti
(1685 - 1757)

Early English Sonatina

William Duncombe
(18th Century)

Air

Henry Purcell
(1658 - 1695)

Bourrée

Christophe Graupner
(1683 - 1760)

Russian Polka

Mikhael Ivanovich Glinka
(1804 - 1857)

Circle Dance

Felix Le Couppey
(1811 - 1887)

Contredanse

Unknown French Composer
(18th Century)

Moderate walking tempo

Rondino Pastorale

Carl Reinecke
(1824 - 1910)

Alexander March

Piano version by
Carl Czerny

Ludwig van Beethoven
(1770 - 1827)

Scherzino

Carl Reinecke
(1824 - 1910)

Rondino

Moderato

Jean Philippe Rameau
(1683 - 1764)

Elegy

Carl Reinecke
(1824 - 1910)

Carnival

François Couperin
(1668 - 1733)

Rigaudon

Georg Philip Telemann

Allegro K.3

Wolfgang Amadeus Mozart
(1756 - 1791)

Allegro giocoso

Solemn Procession

Ignaz Pleyel
(1757 - 1831)

Rondoletto

Christian Traugott Brunner
(1792 - 1874)

Allegretto

Carillons

Johann Philipp Kirnberger
(1721 - 1783)

King William's March

Jeremiah Clarke
(1659 - 1707)

Canzone

Daniel Gottlob Türk
(1756 - 1813)

Andantino

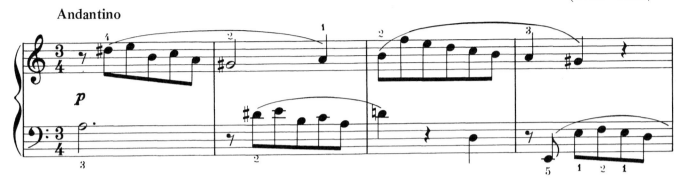

Ländler

Franz Schubert
(1797 - 1828)

Little Piece
from Album For The Young

Robert Schumann
(1810 - 1856)

L'épineuse*

The Thorny One

François Couperin
(1668 - 1733)

* Theme and First Couplet

D.C. al Fine

Arioso

Georg Philipp Telemann
(1681 - 1767)

Repeat **p**

Segue Burlesca

Burlesca

Georg Philipp Telemann

Sonatina No. 2

1st Movement

Jean (T.) Latour
(1766 - 1837)

Gigue

Johann Nikolaus Tischer
(1731 - 1767)

Dance Sonatina

Thomas Attwood
(1763 - 1838)

Romantic Story

Cornelius Gurlitt
(1820 - 1901)

Andantino

Playful Dialogue

Johann Nepomuk Hummel
(1778 - 1837)

Waltz

Franz Schubert
(1797 - 1828)

Moderato

Ecossaise

Friedrich Kuhlau
(1786 - 1832)

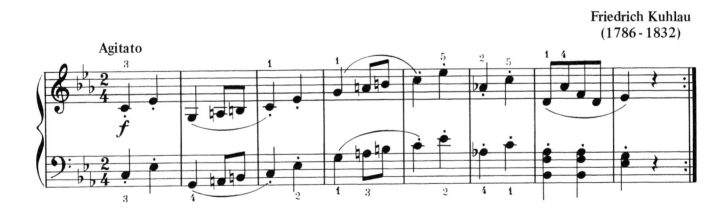

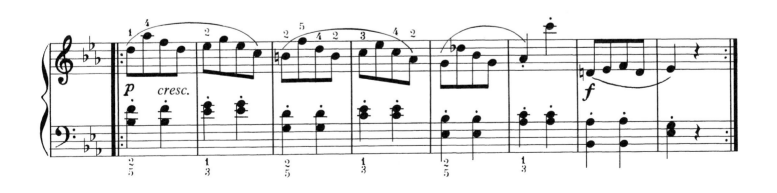

Album Leaf

Franz Liszt
(1811 - 1886)